The Bernard and Irene Schwartz Series on American Competitiveness

The Economic Logic of Illegal Immigration

Gordon H. Hanson

CSR NO. 26, APRIL 2007
COUNCIL ON FOREIGN RELATIONS

Founded in 1921, the Council on Foreign Relations is an independent, national membership organization and a nonpartisan center for scholars dedicated to producing and disseminating ideas so that individual and corporate members, as well as policymakers, journalists, students, and interested citizens in the United States and other countries, can better understand the world and the foreign policy choices facing the United States and other governments. The Council does this by convening meetings; conducting a wide-ranging Studies Program; publishing *Foreign Affairs*, the preeminent journal covering international affairs and U.S. foreign policy; maintaining a diverse membership; sponsoring Independent Task Forces and Special Reports; and providing up-to-date information about the world and U.S. foreign policy on the Council's website, CFR.org.

THE COUNCIL TAKES NO INSTITUTIONAL POSITION ON POLICY ISSUES AND HAS NO AFFILIATION WITH THE U.S. GOVERNMENT. ALL STATEMENTS OF FACT AND EXPRESSIONS OF OPINION CONTAINED IN ITS PUBLICATIONS ARE THE SOLE RESPONSIBILITY OF THE AUTHOR OR AUTHORS.

Council Special Reports (CSRs) are concise policy briefs, produced to provide a rapid response to a developing crisis or contribute to the public's understanding of current policy dilemmas. CSRs are written by individual authors—who may be Council fellows or acknowledged experts from outside the institution—in consultation with an advisory committee, and are intended to take sixty days or less from inception to publication. The committee serves as a sounding board and provides feedback on a draft report. It usually meets twice—once before a draft is written and once again when there is a draft for review; however, advisory committee members, unlike Task Force members, are not asked to sign off on the report or to otherwise endorse it. Once published, CSRs are posted on the Council's website, CFR.org.

Council Special Reports in the Bernard and Irene Schwartz Series on American Competitiveness explore challenges to the long-term health of the U.S. economy. In a globalizing world, the prosperity of American firms and workers is ever more directly affected by critical government policy choices in areas such as spending, taxation, trade, immigration, and intellectual property rights. The reports in the Bernard and Irene Schwartz series analyze the major issues affecting American economic competitiveness and help policymakers identify the concrete steps they can take to promote it.

For further information about the Council or this report, please write to the Council on Foreign Relations, 58 East 68th Street, New York, NY 10021, or call the Communications office at 212-434-9400. Visit our website, CFR.org.

To submit a letter in response to a Council Special Report for publication on our website, CFR.org, you may send an email to CSReditor@cfr.org. Alternatively, letters may be mailed to us at: Publications Department, Council on Foreign Relations, 58 East 68th Street, New York, NY 10021. Letters should include the writer's name, postal address, and daytime phone number. Letters may be edited for length and clarity, and may be published online. Please do not send attachments. All letters become the property of the Council on Foreign Relations and will not be returned. We regret that, owing to the volume of correspondence, we cannot respond to every letter.

CONTENTS

FOREWORD

Immigration reform is one of the most divisive issues confronting U.S. policymakers. The rise in the number of illegal immigrants in the United States over the past ten years—from five to twelve million—has led to concerns about the effects of illegal immigration on wages and public finances, as well as the potential security threats posed by unauthorized entry into the country. In the past year alone, the governors of New Mexico and Arizona have declared a "state of emergency" over illegal immigration, and President Bush signed into law the Secure Fence Act, which authorizes the spending of $1.2 billion for the construction of a seven-hundred-mile fence along the U.S.-Mexico border.

In this Council Special Report, Professor Gordon H. Hanson of the University of California, San Diego approaches immigration through the lens of economics. The results are surprising. By focusing on the economic costs and benefits of legal and illegal immigration, Professor Hanson concludes that stemming illegal immigration would likely lead to a net drain on the U.S. economy—a finding that calls into question many of the proposals to increase funding for border protection. Moreover, Hanson argues that guest worker programs now being considered by Congress fail to account for the economic incentives that drive illegal immigration, which benefits both the undocumented workers who desire to work and live in the United States and employers who want flexible, low-cost labor. Hanson makes the case that unless policymakers design a system of legal immigration that reflects the economic advantages of illegal labor, such programs will not significantly reduce illegal immigration. He concludes with guidelines crucial to any such redesign of U.S. laws and policy. In short, Professor Hanson has written a report that will challenge much of the wisdom (conventional and otherwise) on the economics behind a critical and controversial issue.

This Council Special Report is part of the Bernard and Irene Schwartz Series on American Competitiveness and was produced by the Council's Maurice R. Greenberg Center for Geoeconomic Studies. The Council and the center are grateful to the Bernard and Irene Schwartz Foundation for its support of this important project.

Richard N. Haass
President
Council on Foreign Relations
April 2007

ACKNOWLEDGMENTS

I am particularly grateful to members of the Council Advisory Committee: Mark A. Anderson, Frank D. Bean, Michael J. Christenson, Jose W. Fernandez, James F. Hollifield, Stephen L. Kass, Moushumi M. Khan, F. Ray Marshall, Susan F. Martin, Prachi Mishra, Robert J. Murray, David Perez, Michael Piore, Gerald L. Warren, and especially the chair, Mark R. Rosenzweig. All of the members of the Advisory Committee made valuable comments on the draft as it progressed, although none are responsible for the opinions expressed in this report.

I am grateful to Douglas Holtz-Eakin, former director of the Council's Maurice R. Greenberg Center for Geoeconomic Studies, for directing this project; to Benn Steil, director of international economics at the Council, for offering me the opportunity to write this Council Special Report; and to James Bergman for his editing and comments on the later drafts. Edward Alden, the Bernard L. Schwartz senior fellow, and Sebastian Mallaby, who succeeded Dr. Holtz-Eakin as director of the Geoeconomics Center, contributed the final edits and comments.

I also thank Council President Richard N. Haass and Director of Studies Gary Samore for their comments. For their efforts in the production and dissemination of this report, I would like to thank Patricia Dorff and Lia Norton in the Publications department and Anya Schmemann and her team in Communications.

Finally, I would like to thank the Bernard and Irene Schwartz Foundation for their generous support of this project.

Gordon H. Hanson

COUNCIL SPECIAL REPORT

INTRODUCTION

Illegal immigration is a source of mounting concern for politicians in the United States. In the past ten years, the U.S. population of illegal immigrants has risen from five million to nearly twelve million, prompting angry charges that the country has lost control over its borders.[1] Congress approved measures last year that have significantly tightened enforcement along the U.S.-Mexico border in an effort to stop the flow of unauthorized migrants, and it is expected to make another effort this year at the first comprehensive reform of immigration laws in more than twenty years.

Legal immigrants, who account for two-thirds of all foreign-born residents in the United States and 50 to 70 percent of net new immigrant arrivals, are less subject to public scrutiny. There is a widely held belief that legal immigration is largely good for the country and illegal immigration is largely bad. Despite intense differences of opinion in Congress, there is a strong consensus that if the United States could simply reduce the number of illegal immigrants in the country, either by converting them into legal residents or deterring them at the border, U.S. economic welfare would be enhanced.

Is there any evidence to support these prevailing views? In terms of the economic benefits and costs, is legal immigration really better than illegal immigration? What should the United States as a country hope to achieve economically through its immigration policies? Are the types of legislative proposals that Congress is considering consistent with these goals?

This Council Special Report addresses the economic logic of the current high levels of illegal immigration. The aim is not to provide a comprehensive review of all the issues involved in immigration, particularly those related to homeland security. Rather, it is to examine the costs, benefits, incentives, and disincentives of illegal immigration

---

[1] Jeffrey S. Passel, "Estimates of the Size and Characteristics of the Undocumented Population," Pew Hispanic Center, 2006. Estimates of the illegal immigrant population are imprecise. They are based on comparing the actual number of immigrants (as enumerated in household population surveys) with the number of immigrants admitted through legal means. The stock of illegal immigrants is taken to be the difference between these two values (after accounting for mortality and return migration). See Jennifer Van Hook, Weiwei Zhang, Frank D. Bean, and Jeffrey S. Passel, "Foreign-Born Emigration: A New Approach and Estimates Based on Matched CPS Files," *Demography*, Vol. 43, No. 2 (May 2006), pp. 361–82, for a discussion of recent academic literature on estimation methods and on how existing estimates of the stock of illegal immigrants may not fully account for emigration among this population.

within the boundaries of economic analysis. From a purely economic perspective, the optimal immigration policy would admit individuals whose skills are in shortest supply and whose tax contributions, net of the cost of public services they receive, are as large as possible. Admitting immigrants in scarce occupations would yield the greatest increase in U.S. incomes, regardless of the skill level of those immigrants. In the United States, scarce workers would include not only highly educated individuals, such as the software programmers and engineers employed by rapidly expanding technology industries, but also low-skilled workers in construction, food preparation, and cleaning services, for which the supply of U.S. native labor has been falling. In either case, the national labor market for these workers is tight, in the sense that U.S. wages for these occupations are high relative to wages abroad.

Of course, the aggregate economic consequences of immigration policy do not account for other important considerations, including the impact of immigration on national security, civil rights, or political life.[2] Illegal immigration has obvious flaws. Continuing high levels of illegal immigration may undermine the rule of law and weaken the ability of the U.S. government to enforce labor-market regulations. There is an understandable concern that massive illegal entry from Mexico heightens U.S. exposure to international terrorism, although no terrorist activity to date has been tied to individuals who snuck across the U.S.-Mexico border.[3] Large inflows of illegal aliens also relax the commitment of employers to U.S. labor-market institutions and create a population of workers with limited upward mobility and an uncertain place in U.S. society. These are obviously valid complaints that deserve a hearing in the debate on immigration policy reform. However, within this debate we hear relatively little about the

---

[2] See Samuel P. Huntington, *Who Are We? The Challenges to America's National Identity* (New York: Simon and Schuster, 2004), and Patrick J. Buchanan, *State of Emergency: The Third World Invasion and Conquest of America* (New York: Thomas Dunne, 2006).

[3] According to Rep. Tom Tancredo (R–CO), a leading congressional opponent of immigration, "There are nine to eleven million illegal aliens living amongst us right now, who have never had a criminal background check and have never been screened through any terrorism databases. Yet the political leadership of this country seems to think that attacking terrorism overseas will allow us to ignore the invitation our open borders presents to those who wish to strike us at home" (http://www.house.gov/tancredo/Immigration/, accessed on October 31, 2006). Former presidential candidate Pat Buchanan adds, "The enemy is already inside the gates. How many others among our eleven million 'undocumented' immigrants are ready to carry out truck bombings, assassinations, sabotage, skyjackings?" ("U.S. Pays the High Price of Empire," *Los Angeles Times*, September 18, 2001.) See also Steven A. Camarota, *The Open Door: How Militant Islamic Terrorists Entered and Remained in the United States*, Center for Immigration Studies Paper No. 21 (2002).

4

actual magnitude of the costs and benefits associated with illegal immigration and how they compare to those for legal inflows.

This analysis concludes that there is little evidence that legal immigration is economically preferable to illegal immigration. In fact, illegal immigration responds to market forces in ways that legal immigration does not. Illegal migrants tend to arrive in larger numbers when the U.S. economy is booming (relative to Mexico and the Central American countries that are the source of most illegal immigration to the United States) and move to regions where job growth is strong. Legal immigration, in contrast, is subject to arbitrary selection criteria and bureaucratic delays, which tend to disassociate legal inflows from U.S. labor-market conditions.[4] Over the last half-century, there appears to be little or no response of legal immigration to the U.S. unemployment rate.[5] Two-thirds of legal permanent immigrants are admitted on the basis of having relatives in the United States. Only by chance will the skills of these individuals match those most in demand by U.S. industries. While the majority of temporary legal immigrants come to the country at the invitation of a U.S. employer, the process of obtaining a visa is often arduous and slow. Once here, temporary legal workers cannot easily move between jobs, limiting their benefit to the U.S. economy.

There are many reasons to be concerned about rising levels of illegal immigration. Yet, as Congress is again this year set to consider the biggest changes to immigration laws in two decades, it is critical not to lose sight of the fact that illegal immigration has a clear economic logic: It provides U.S. businesses with the types of workers they want, when they want them, and where they want them. If policy reform succeeds in making U.S. illegal immigrants more like legal immigrants, in terms of their skills, timing of arrival, and occupational mobility, it is likely to lower rather than raise national welfare. In their efforts to gain control over illegal immigration, Congress and the administration need to be cautious that the economic costs do not outstrip the putative benefits.

---

[4] Susan Martin, "U.S. Employment-Based Admissions: Permanent and Temporary," Migration Policy Institute Policy Brief No. 15 (January 2006).

[5] James Hollifield and Valerie F. Hunt find that, over the period of 1891–1945, there is a negative correlation between U.S. legal immigration and the U.S. unemployment rate, indicating that immigrant inflows are larger when U.S. labor markets are tighter. After 1945, this relationship breaks down. See James F. Hollifield and Valerie F. Hunt, "Immigrants, Markets, and Rights: The US as an Emerging Migration State," paper prepared for presentation at the Migration Ethnicity Meeting (MEM) at IZA in Bonn, Germany, May 13–16, 2006.

CURRENT U.S. IMMIGRATION POLICY

For a foreign citizen, there are three options to live and work in the United States: Become a legal permanent resident, obtain a temporary work visa, or enter the country illegally and remain here as an unauthorized immigrant. In 2005, there were thirty-five million immigrants living in the United States, of which 30 percent were in the country illegally and 3 percent were temporary legal residents (Figure 1).[6] The foreign-born now make up 12 percent of the U.S. population. Each type of immigration—legal permanent, temporary legal, and illegal—is subject to its own set of admission policies and behavioral restrictions.

Figure 1: The U.S. Immigrant Population

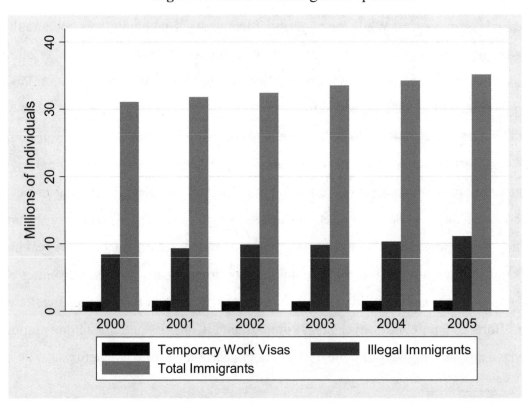

Source: U.S. Census Bureau (http://www.census.gov/); Passel, "Estimates of the Size and Characteristics of the Undocumented Population."

---

[6] The total number of immigrants is from the U.S. Census Bureau (http://www.census.gov/); the numbers of temporary legal immigrants and illegal immigrants are from Passel, "Estimates of the Size and Characteristics of the Undocumented Population."

The United States awards visas for legal permanent residence, or green cards, based on a quota system established by the Hart-Celler Immigration Bill of 1965. Hart-Celler made family reunification a central feature of U.S. admission decisions. The U.S. government assigns applicants for green cards to one of several categories, each subject to its own quota. The law guarantees admission to immediate family members of U.S. citizens, who are exempt from entry quotas. Specific quotas are assigned to other family members of U.S. citizens, immediate family members of legal U.S. residents, individuals with special skills, refugees and asylees facing persecution in their home countries, and a few other categories.[7] Applicants must be sponsored by a U.S. citizen or legal resident.

The granting of visas is biased in favor of applicants with family members in the United States. Of the 958,000 legal permanent immigrants admitted in 2004, 66 percent gained entry under preferences for family-sponsored immigrants, 16 percent gained entry under preferences for employer-sponsored immigrants, 7 percent were refugees or asylees, 5 percent were diversity immigrants (from countries underrepresented in previous admissions), and 5 percent were admitted under other categories.[8] There is often a long lag between applying for a green card and receipt of a visa, with delays in excess of five years common.[9]

By no means are all individuals receiving green cards new arrivals in the United States. In 2004, 61 percent of green card recipients were individuals already residing in the country, either as temporary legal immigrants or illegal aliens. Many illegal or temporary legal immigrants currently in the United States have applied for legal permanent residence and will ultimately receive a green card. For these immigrants, their initial immigration status is the first step on a path to becoming a U.S. legal permanent resident. The large numbers of transitions from temporary to legal permanent residence

---

[7] The Immigration Act of 1990 set a flexible cap for legal admissions at 675,000, of which 480,000 would be family-based, 140,000 would be employment-based, and 55,000 would be diversity immigrants. The law also set temporary immigration for the H-1 and H-2 programs and created new categories for temporary workers (O, P, Q, R). Subsequent legislation created categories for temporary immigration of professional workers from countries that have a free-trade agreement with the United States. See U.S. Department of Homeland Security, "2005 Yearbook of Immigration Statistics," Office of Immigration Statistics, 2006.

[8] In 2005, the number of green card recipients was 1.1 million, an increase over 2004 due in part to the U.S. government allowing for a one time increase in employer-sponsored admissions (to compensate for employer-sponsored visas that had gone unfilled in earlier years, as seen in Figure 4).

[9] David A. Martin, "Twilight Statuses: A Closer Examination of the Unauthorized Population," Migration Policy Institute Policy Brief No. 2 (June 2005).

and from illegal to legal status that suggest distinctions between legal permanent immigration and other types of inflows are less clear cut than one might think.

After five years as a legal permanent resident, an immigrant is eligible to apply for U.S. citizenship. Citizenship confers the right to vote and the right to draw on all government benefit programs for which an individual is eligible. In 1996, Congress excluded noncitizens from access to many government entitlement programs.[10] In effect, those receiving a green card now have to wait five years before they are eligible to participate in most types of means-tested entitlement programs. However, the Supreme Court has ruled the government may not deny public education or emergency medical services to any foreign-born U.S. resident, legal or illegal.

Temporary immigration visas permit foreign citizens to work in the United States for a designated period of time. These visas go to temporary workers, investors from countries with which the United States has a free trade treaty, and intracompany transferees.[11] In 2005, such visas allowed 1.6 million such individuals and their families to enter the country.[12] About half of those admissions are for temporary workers and their family members. Each year, the United States makes available sixty-five thousand new three-year visas for high-skilled workers under the H-1B program and sixty-six thousand one-year visas available under the H-2A and H-2B programs. The H-1B visa applies mainly to workers in high-tech industries. It was created in 1990 to permit foreigners with a college degree to work in the United States for a renewable three-year term for employers who petition on their behalf. The H-2A visa applies to seasonal laborers in agriculture; the H-2B visa applies to seasonal manual laborers in construction, tourism, and other nonagricultural activities. Other temporary work visas go to workers with extraordinary abilities, athletes, artists, and workers in religious occupations.

Except for the H-2 visas, which typically account for less than 10 percent of the total, the vast majority of temporary work visas go to individuals with high levels of education or in highly specialized occupations. The conditions applied to these visas

---

[10] Many states have since restored access of noncitizens to some benefits, according to Wendy Zimmerman and Karen C. Tumlin, "Patchwork Policies: State Assistance for Immigrants under Welfare Reform," Urban Institute Paper No. 21 (April 1999).

[11] Other temporary entry visas go to tourists, aliens in transit, exchange visitors, students, representatives of foreign media, foreign government officials, and foreign representatives of international organizations. Of these, the last four groups are permitted to work in the United States under restricted conditions.

[12] DHS, "2005 Yearbook."

make it difficult for most temporary workers to switch employers once in the United States. Many employers resort to an H-1B visa when they are unable to obtain an employer-sponsored green card for a foreign-born worker they would like to hire. This suggests there is a link between H-1B visas and employer-sponsored permanent immigration, in that decreases in the supply of visas for one of these categories are likely to increase demand for the other.

Though the United States does not set the level of illegal immigration explicitly, existing enforcement policies effectively permit substantial numbers of illegal aliens to enter the country. In 2005, the illegal immigrant population was estimated to be 11.1 million individuals, up from five million in 1996 and 8.4 million in 2000.[13] Most illegal immigrants come to the United States by crossing the U.S.-Mexico border or overstaying temporary entry visas. The U.S. Border Patrol tries to prevent illegal immigration by policing the U.S.-Mexico border and other points of entry from abroad. While the border patrol has monitored the border in an effort to halt illegal entry since the agency was created in 1924, the modern experience of high illegal immigration dates back only to the 1970s, following the end of the *Bracero* program (1942–1964), which allowed seasonal farm laborers from Mexico and the Caribbean to work in U.S. agriculture on a temporary basis.[14] Initially, illegal immigrants were concentrated in agriculture; today, they are more likely to work in construction, low-end manufacturing, cleaning services, or food preparation.[15]

Current U.S. policy on illegal immigration is based largely on the Immigration Reform and Control Act (IRCA) of 1986, which made it illegal to employ undocumented workers, mandated monitoring of employers, and expanded border enforcement.[16] IRCA

---

[13] Passel, "Estimates of the Size and Characteristics of the Undocumented Population."

[14] The U.S. Congress enacted the *Bracero* program in response to the labor crunch associated with World War II, according to Kitty Calavita, *Inside the State: The Bracero Program, Immigration and the INS* (Routledge, Chapman and Hall, 1992). The program remained in place for two decades after the war, despite intense opposition from organized labor. U.S. employers were allowed to bring in workers from Mexico and the Caribbean to fulfill short-term labor contracts. At the end of their contracts, workers were required to return to their home countries. The vast majority of *braceros* worked on U.S. farms. At its peak, from 1954 to 1960, 300,000 to 450,000 temporary migrant workers entered the United States annually. The end of the *Bracero* program marked the beginning of large-scale illegal immigration from Mexico, creating the perception that terminating temporary immigration induced U.S. employers to seek out illegal labor.

[15] Passel, "Estimates of the Size and Characteristics of the Undocumented Population."

[16] The Illegal Immigration Reform and Immigrant Responsibility Act of 1996 further expanded resources for border enforcement and made it easier to deport illegal aliens and criminal aliens.

also offered amnesty to illegal aliens who had resided in the United States since before 1982 (with shorter residency requirements for agricultural workers). As a result of IRCA, the United States granted legal permanent residence to 2.7 million individuals, two million of whom were Mexican nationals.[17]

Over time, the border patrol has sharply stepped up enforcement. Between 1990 and 2005, the number of officer hours spent policing the U.S.-Mexico border increased by 2.9 times. In 2004, immigration authorities apprehended 1.2 million illegal aliens in the United States, 95 percent of whom were caught on or near the U.S.-Mexico border.[18] Most border patrol activities are concentrated in U.S. cities that border Mexico, which has encouraged illegal immigrants to cross in the less populated—and more treacherous—desert and mountain regions of Arizona, California, and Texas.[19] Currently, there is relatively little enforcement against illegal immigration at U.S. worksites. Employers are required to ask prospective employees for proof of employment eligibility (typically in the form of a Social Security card and a green card). As long as the proffered documentation appears legitimate, an employer is plausibly able to deny having knowingly hired any illegal aliens.[20]

Together, U.S. immigrants constitute a diverse group. Relative to the native-born U.S. population, they are disproportionately concentrated at the low and high ends of the skill distribution (Figure 2). One-third of immigrants have less than a high school education, compared to just 12 percent of U.S. natives, and one-fifth have less than a ninth grade education, compared to just 4 percent of U.S. natives. At the other extreme, one-quarter of immigrants hold a bachelor's or advanced degree. While most U.S. native

---

[17] Bureau of International Labor Affairs, *Effects of the Immigration Reform and Control Act: Characteristics and Labor Market Behavior of the Legalized Population Five Years Following Legalization* (Washington, DC: U.S. Department of Labor, 1996).

[18] Apprehensions of illegal aliens overstate attempted illegal immigration as the border patrol may capture a single individual multiple times in a given year.

[19] Wayne A. Cornelius, "Death at the Border: Efficacy and Unintended Consequences of U.S. Immigration Control Policy," *Population and Development Review*, Vol. 27, No. 4 (December 2001), pp. 661–85.

[20] Between 1999 and 2003, the number of man hours U.S. immigration agents devoted to worksite inspections declined from 480,000 (or 9 percent of total agent hours) to 180,000 hours (or 4 percent of total agent hours). Few U.S. employers who hire illegal immigrants are detected or prosecuted. The number of U.S. employers paying fines of at least $5,000 for hiring unauthorized workers was only fifteen in 1990, which fell to twelve in 1994 and to zero in 2004. Since September 11, 2001, the majority of worksite enforcement has been devoted to monitoring designated critical infrastructure sites, such as airports and power plants, according to the U.S. Government Accountability Office, "Immigration Enforcement: Preliminary Observations on Employment Verification and Worksite Enforcement," GAO-05-822T (June 21, 2005).

workers have intermediate levels of education (a high school degree or some college), these categories account for a relatively small share of immigrants.

Figure 2: Educational Attainment of Immigrants and Natives, 2004

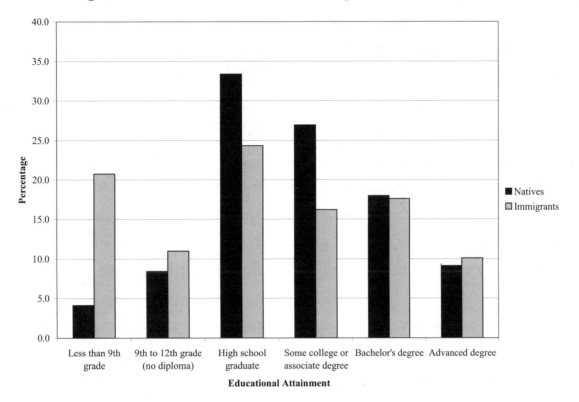

Source: U.S. Census, Current Population Survey 2003 (URL: http://www.census.gov/population/www/socdemo/education/cps2003.html).

Different types of immigration produce very different types of immigrants. With the exception of manual laborers on H-2 visas, most temporary legal immigrants are highly skilled.[21] Among legal permanent immigrants, those entering under employment-based preferences are also highly skilled, with 30 percent of these individuals having a college degree and another 38 percent having a postgraduate degree.[22] Family-based legal permanent immigrants appear to have lower education levels. Illegal immigrants appear

---

[21] DHS, "2005 Yearbook."
[22] Guillermina Jasso and Mark R. Rosenzweig, "Selection Criteria and the Skill Composition of Immigrants: A Comparative Analysis of Australian and US Employment Immigration" (mimeo, New York University and Yale University, 2005).

to have the lowest education levels and to be the most concentrated in low-wage occupations, such as construction, food preparation, cleaning services, and agriculture.[23]

Education and skill are not all that distinguish legal and illegal immigrants. Inflows of illegal immigrants tend to be highly sensitive to economic conditions, with inflows rising during periods when the U.S. economy is expanding and Mexico's is contracting. Examining month-to-month changes in apprehensions of illegal immigrants attempting to cross the U.S.-Mexico border reveals that when Mexican wages fall by 10 percent relative to U.S. wages, attempts at illegal entry increase by 6 percent.[24] The responsiveness of illegal immigration to economic conditions is to be expected. These individuals come to the United States seeking work and their incentive to do so is strongest when the difference in job prospects on the two sides of the border is greatest. The illegal immigrant population is also quite mobile geographically within the United States. During the 1990s, U.S. job growth was strongest in mountain states and the southeast. These states also registered the largest percentage increases in the number of illegal immigrants.[25]

Legal immigration, in contrast, responds to economic conditions more slowly. Annual quotas for green cards are fixed and clearing the queue for a green card requires several years or more, making legal permanent immigration insensitive to the U.S. business cycle. Quotas for temporary legal immigration do change over time but do not track the U.S. economy with much precision. Relative to illegal immigrants, temporary legal immigrants are far less mobile, as most work visas are tied to a particular employer.[26] Visa holders cannot change jobs without employer approval.

The flexibility and mobility of illegal immigrants may in part reflect the informal employment relationships to which many are subject. In construction, employers hire

---

[23] On education levels, see Gordon H. Hanson, "Illegal Migration from Mexico to the United States," *Journal of Economic Literature*, Vol. 44, No. 4 (December 2006), pp. 869–924. On occupations, see Passel, "Estimates of the Size and Characteristics of the Undocumented Population."

[24] Gordon H. Hanson and Antonio Spilimbergo, "Illegal Immigration, Border Enforcement, and Relative Wages: Evidence from Apprehensions at the U.S.-Mexico Border," *American Economic Review*, Vol. 89, No. 5 (December 1999), pp. 1337–57.

[25] See David Card and Ethan G. Lewis, "The Diffusion of Mexican Immigrants During the 1990s: Explanations and Impacts," in George J. Borjas, ed., *Mexican Immigration to the United States* (Chicago: University of Chicago Press, 2007) and Passel, "Estimates of the Size and Characteristics of the Undocumented Population."

[26] Martin, "U.S. Employment-Based Admissions."

illegal immigrants for a specific job, with no promise of employment after the project is completed. Similar arrangements exist in agriculture, where illegal immigrants who work on a farm for one growing season may or may not be invited to return the following year. In housecleaning, child care, or food preparation, the demand for illegal labor may be less seasonal in nature but employment relationships are not necessarily more secure. Illegal immigrants are typically contracted on an at-will basis, without a legal contract that defines the terms and conditions of their jobs. The informality of illegal employment contributes to the flexibility of illegal labor markets.

ILLEGAL IMMIGRATION AND THE U.S. ECONOMY

For a given labor inflow, the productivity gains from immigration will be larger the scarcer the skills of the incoming immigrants. A given type of worker may be scarce either because the U.S. supply of his skill type is low relative to the rest of the world, as with workers who have little schooling, or because the U.S. demand for his skill type is high relative to the rest of the world, as with computer scientists and engineers.

Due to steady increases in high school completion rates, native-born U.S. workers with low schooling levels are increasingly hard to find. Yet these workers are an important part of the U.S. economy—they build homes, prepare food, clean offices, harvest crops, and take unfilled factory jobs. Between 1960 and 2000, the share of working-age native-born U.S. residents with less than twelve years of schooling fell from 50 percent to 12 percent. Abroad, low-skilled workers are more abundant. In Mexico, as of 2000, 74 percent of working-age residents had less than twelve years of education. Migration from Mexico to the United States moves individuals from a country where their relative abundance leaves them with low productivity and low wages to a country where their relative scarcity allows them to command much higher earnings. For a twenty-five-year-old Mexican male with nine years of education (slightly above the national average), migrating to the United States would increase his wage from $2.30 to $8.50 an hour, adjusted for cost of living differences in the two countries.[27] While the net economic impact of immigration on the U.S. economy may be small (as discussed below), the gains to immigrant households from moving to the United States are enormous.

For low-skilled workers in much of the world, U.S. admission policies make illegal immigration the most viable means of entering the country. In 2005, 56 percent of illegal immigrants were Mexican nationals. Given low average schooling, few Mexican citizens qualify for employment-based green cards or most types of temporary work visas (Figure 3).[28] Family-based immigration visas have queues that are too long and

---

[27] Hanson, "Illegal Migration from Mexico to the United States."
[28] Family-sponsored immigration accounts for over 90 percent of Mexican nationals who gain legal permanent residence in the United States (DHS, "2005 Yearbook").

14

admission criteria that are too arbitrary to serve most prospective migrants who would like to work in the United States in the immediate future. As a consequence, most Mexican immigrants enter the United States illegally. Although many ultimately obtain green cards, they remain unauthorized for a considerable period of time. The Pew Hispanic Center estimates that in 2005 80 to 85 percent of Mexican immigrants who had been in the United States less than ten years were unauthorized.[29] Illegal immigration thus accomplishes what legal immigration does not: It moves large numbers of low-skilled workers from a low-productivity to a high-productivity environment.

Figure 3: Mexican Immigrants in the United States

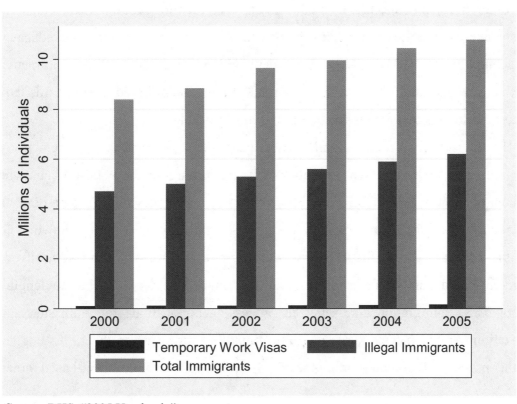

Source: DHS, "2005 Yearbook."

Illegal immigration also brings low-skilled workers to the United States when the productivity gains of doing so appear to be highest. During the past twenty years, Mexico has experienced several severe economic contractions, with emigration from the country spiking in the aftermath of each downturn. In terms of the economic benefits, this is

---

[29] Passel, "Estimates of the Size and Characteristics of the Undocumented Population."

exactly when one would want workers to move—when their labor productivity in the United States is highest relative to their labor productivity at home. Long queues for U.S. green cards mean there is little way for legal permanent immigration to respond to such changes in international economic conditions.

For high-skilled labor, legal immigration is the primary means of entering the United States. Compared to the rest of the world, the United States has an abundant supply of highly educated labor. One might expect that, if anything, skilled labor would want to leave the country rather than try to move here. However, over the past two decades the U.S. economy has enjoyed rapid advances in new technology, which have increased the demand for highly skilled labor.[30] The spread of information technology, among other developments, has created demand for software programmers, electrical engineers, and other skilled technicians. Even with the abundant U.S. supply of educated labor, technology-induced increases in labor demand have made the country an attractive destination for educated workers from abroad. Employment-based green cards and temporary work visas make such skilled immigration possible.

By the scarcity criterion, skills-based permanent immigration and temporary immigration admit the right type of labor. Yet, the timing of these inflows and the subsequent occupational immobility of many of these workers leave much to be desired. Employment-based permanent immigration moves erratically over time, showing no discernible correlation with the U.S. employment rate (Figure 4).[31] The volatility of employment-based admissions is due not to economic considerations but to lengthy delays by U.S. immigration authorities in processing applications for admission and naturalization. An unexpected surge in applications for citizenship in the 1990s bogged down the process of granting immigration visas, including employment-based green

---

[30] Lawrence F. Katz and David H. Autor, "Changes in the Wage Structure and Earnings Inequality," in Orley Ashenfelter and David Card, eds., *Handbook of Labor Economics, Vol. 3A* (Amsterdam: Elsevier Science, 1999), pp. 1463–1555.

[31] Figure 4 shows admissions of individuals to the United States on employer-sponsored legal permanent resident visas (DHS, "2005 Yearbook") and the stock of individuals on H1-B visas, which has been calculated using data on the number of H1-B visas issued in B. Lindsay Lowell, "H-1B Temporary Workers: Estimating the Population" (mimeo, Institute for the Study of International Migration, Georgetown University, 2000), and from the U.S. Department of State Office of Visa Statistics (http://travel.state.gov/visa/frvi/statistics/). The stock equals the sum of the current and preceding two years of visa issuances (since H1-B visas are valid for three years), assuming that in each year 2 percent of visa holders die and 50 percent return home. Values for mortality and emigration rates are taken from Lowell, "H-1B Temporary Workers."

cards, leading to a fall in the number of highly skilled immigrants receiving legal permanent residence visas.[32] Ironically, the reduction in employment-based admissions occurred during the height of the 1990s technology boom. Temporary immigration of skilled workers tracks the U.S. economy somewhat more closely. The number of H-1B visas fell behind U.S. employment growth in the early 1990s, surged ahead during the late stages of the 1990s boom, and then lost strength in the early 2000s after the economy slowed briefly and then resumed growth. Far from leading U.S. expansions, temporary work visas have lagged employment growth by two to three years.

Figure 4: Immigration and the Rate of Employment, 1990–2005

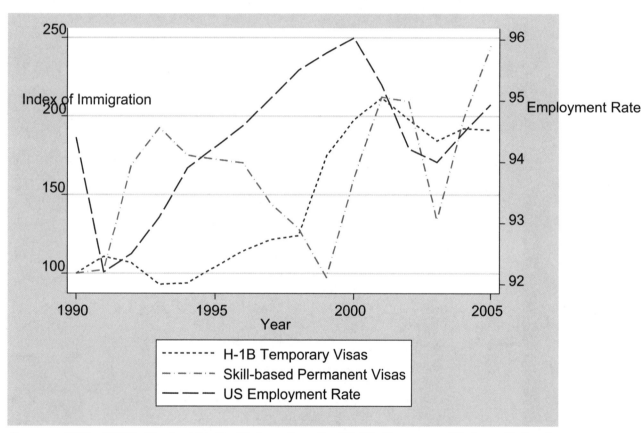

Sources: DHS, "2005 Yearbook"; B. Lindsay Lowell, "H-1B Temporary Workers: Estimating the Population" (mimeo, Institute for the Study of International Migration, Georgetown University, 2000); and U.S. Department of State Office of Visa Statistics (http://travel.state.gov/visa/frvi/statistics/). For further information on calculation of values, see footnote 31.

---

[32] DHS, "2005 Yearbook."

Illegal immigration, employment-based permanent immigration, and temporary immigration each tend to provide the U.S. economy with workers who are in scarce supply. Family-based immigration, which is the largest component of permanent admissions, is set without regard to U.S. labor market conditions. Legal immigration of skilled workers is hindered by queues for visas and lags in adjusting visa levels, which reduce the economic value of such immigration. Flows of illegal immigrants, in contrast, are closely tied to U.S. and Mexican business cycles.

BENEFITS AND COSTS OF IMMIGRATION

Are the gains that illegal immigration brings in terms of labor market flexibility offset by other economic costs? Critics of illegal immigration argue that an influx of illegal immigrants brings high economic costs by lowering domestic wages and raising expenditures on public services such as health care and education. If those costs are sufficiently high, the economic case for restricting illegal immigration would be strengthened.

Overall, immigration increases the incomes of U.S. residents by allowing the economy to utilize domestic resources more efficiently. But because immigrants of different types—illegal, legal temporary, and legal permanent—have varying skill levels, income-earning ability, family size, and rights to use public services, changes in their respective inflows have different economic impacts. Immigration also affects U.S. incomes through its impact on tax revenue and public expenditure. Immigrants with lower incomes and larger families tend to be a bigger drain on public spending. Immigrants pay income, payroll, sales, property, and other taxes, with lower-skilled immigrants making smaller contributions. Immigrants use public services by sending their kids to public schools, demanding fire and police protection, driving on roads and highways, and receiving public assistance, with families that have larger numbers of children absorbing more expenditure. Adding the pretax income gains from immigration to immigrants' net tax contributions—their tax payments less the value of government services they use—allows for a rough estimate of the net impact of immigration on the U.S. economy.

Immigration generates extra income for the U.S. economy, even as it pushes down wages for some workers. By increasing the supply of labor, immigration raises the productivity of resources that are complementary to labor. More workers allow U.S. capital, land, and natural resources to be exploited more efficiently. Increasing the supply of labor to perishable fruits and vegetables, for instance, means that each acre of land under cultivation generates more output. Similarly, an expansion in the number of manufacturing workers allows the existing industrial base to produce more goods. The gain in productivity yields extra income for U.S. businesses, which is termed the immigration surplus. The annual immigration surplus in the United States appears to be small, equal to about 0.2 percent of GDP in 2004.[33]

These benefits, however, are not shared equally. Labor inflows from abroad redistribute income away from workers who compete with immigrants in the labor market. George Borjas estimates that over the period 1980 to 2000 immigration contributed to a decrease in average U.S. wages of 3 percent.[34] This estimate accounts for the total change in the U.S. labor force due to immigration, including both legal and illegal sources. Since immigration is concentrated among the low-skilled, low-skilled natives are the workers most likely to be hurt. Over the 1980 to 2000 period, wages of native workers without a high school degree fell by 9 percent as a result of immigration.[35] On the other hand, lower wages for low-skilled labor mean lower prices for labor-intensive goods and services, especially those whose prices are set in local markets rather than through competition in global markets. Patricia Cortes finds that in the 1980s and 1990s U.S. cities with larger inflows of low-skilled immigrants experienced larger reductions in prices for housekeeping, gardening, child care, dry cleaning, and other labor-intensive, locally traded services.[36] Lower prices for goods and services raise the

---

[33] The formula for the immigration surplus, expressed as a share of GDP (in 2004), is given by -0.5 times the product of labor's share of national income (0.7), the square of the fraction of the labor force that is foreign-born (the ratio 21.2 million/146.1 million squared), and the percentage change in wages due to a one-percent increase in the labor force (0.3). See George J. Borjas, *Heaven's Door: Immigration Policy and the American Economy* (Princeton, NJ: Princeton University Press, 1999). Estimates of the immigration surplus should be viewed with caution, as this calculation treats labor as homogeneous and ignores the consequences of immigration for capital accumulation and technological innovation. Even incorporating such considerations, it would be difficult to produce a plausible estimate of the immigration surplus that was much larger than a fraction of one percent of U.S. GDP.

[34] George J. Borjas, "The Labor Demand Curve is Downward Sloping: Reexamining the Impact of Immigration on the Labor Market," *Quarterly Journal of Economics*, Vol. 118, No. 4 (June 2003), pp. 1335–74. This wage impact should be viewed as temporary. In the long run, one would expect immigration to raise the incentive for capital accumulation, which could negate immigration's impact on wages. Other research suggests that the wage consequences of immigration are minimal—see David Card, "Is the New Immigration Really So Bad?" NBER Working Paper No. 11547 (August 2005). Were this the case, the immigration surplus would be even smaller than the above estimates suggest.

[35] Consistent with these effects, Kenneth F. Scheve and Matthew J. Slaughter find that opposition to immigration in the United States is most intense among native workers with less than a high school degree. See Kenneth F. Scheve and Matthew J. Slaughter, *Globalization and the Perceptions of American Workers* (Washington, DC: Institute for International Economics, 2001).

[36] Patricia Cortes, "The Effect of Low-Skilled Immigration on U.S. Prices: Evidence from CPI Data" (mimeo, MIT, November 2005). Based on her estimates, a 10 percent increase in the local immigrant population is associated with decreases in prices for labor-intensive services of 1.3 percent and other non-traded goods of 0.2 percent.

real incomes of U.S. households, with most of these gains going to those in regions with large immigrant populations.

Immigration, by admitting large numbers of low-skilled individuals, may exacerbate inefficiencies associated with the country's system of public finance.[37] If immigrants pay more in taxes than they receive in government benefits, then immigration generates a net fiscal transfer to native taxpayers. The total impact of immigration on U.S. residents—the sum of the immigration surplus (the pretax income gain) and the net fiscal transfer from immigrants—would be unambiguously positive. This appears to be the case for immigrants with high skill levels, suggesting that employment-based permanent immigrants and highly skilled temporary immigrants have a positive net impact on the U.S. economy.[38] They generate a positive immigration surplus (by raising U.S. productivity) and make a positive net tax contribution (by adding to U.S. government coffers).[39]

On the other hand, if immigrants pay less in taxes than they receive in government benefits, then immigration generates a net fiscal burden on native taxpayers—native households would be making an income transfer to immigrant households. Paying for this fiscal transfer would require tax increases on natives, reductions in government benefits to natives, or increased borrowing from future generations (by issuing government debt). If immigrants are a net fiscal drain, the total impact of immigration on the United States would be positive only if the immigration surplus exceeded the fiscal transfer made to immigrants. For low-skilled immigration, whether legal or illegal, this does not appear to be the case.[40]

---

[37] Also, immigration-induced population growth may worsen distortions due to poorly defined property rights over air, water, and public spaces. More people means more pollution and more congestion.

[38] James P. Smith and Barry Edmonston, eds., *The New Americans: Economic, Demographic, and Fiscal Effects of Immigration* (Washington, DC: National Academies Press, 1997).

[39] An additional potential benefit from immigration is that it may help the government manage unfunded pension liabilities. See Alan J. Auerbach and Philip Oreopoulos, "Analyzing the Fiscal Impact of U.S. Immigration," *American Economic Review*, Vol. 89, No. 2 (May 1999), pp. 176–180.

[40] See Smith and Edmonston, *The New Americans*; and Steven A. Camarota, *The High Cost of Cheap Labor: Illegal Immigration and the Federal Budget* (Center for Immigration Studies, 2004). Illegal immigrants do contribute to tax revenues. They pay sales taxes on their consumption purchases and property taxes on dwellings they own or rent. In addition, many contribute to Social Security and federal and state income taxes. As of 1986, U.S. law requires employers to record the Social Security number and visa information of each immigrant employee. Many illegal immigrants present employers with Social Security cards that have invalid numbers. Between 1986 and 2000, annual Social Security contributions with invalid numbers rose from $7 billion to $49 billion (Social Security Administration, 2003). While the Social Security

Calculating the fiscal consequences of immigration, while straightforward conceptually, is difficult in practice. To estimate correctly, one needs to know many details about the income, spending, and employment behavior of the entire population of immigrants. As a result, there are few comprehensive national level analyses of the fiscal impact of immigration. The National Research Council (NRC) has conducted detailed fiscal case studies on immigration in New Jersey and California, which have relatively large immigrant populations.[41] In 2000, a few years after the study was conducted, the share of the foreign-born adult population was 34 percent in California and 24 percent in New Jersey, compared with 15 percent in the nation as a whole. The two states have immigrant populations with quite different skill profiles and patterns of welfare usage. In 2000, the share of immigrant households headed by someone with less than a high school education was 34 percent in California and 29 percent in the nation as a whole, but only 23 percent in New Jersey. Similarly, the share of immigrant households receiving cash benefits from welfare programs was 13 percent in California and 10 percent in the nation as a whole, but only 8 percent in New Jersey. These differences in welfare uptake are due in part to immigrants in California being less skilled and in part to California offering more generous benefits.

Based on federal, state, and local government expenditures and tax receipts, the NRC estimated that the short-run fiscal impact of immigration was negative in both New Jersey and California. In New Jersey, using data for 1989–1990, immigrant households received an average net fiscal transfer from natives of $1,500, or 3 percent of average state immigrant household income. Spread among the more numerous state native population, this amounted to an average net fiscal burden of $230 per native household, or 0.4 percent of average state native household income. In California, using data for 1994–95, immigrant households received an average net fiscal transfer of $3,500, or 9 percent of average immigrant household income, which resulted in an average fiscal burden on native households of $1,200, or 2 percent of average native household income. The impact of immigration on California is more negative because immigrant households in the state (a) are more numerous relative to the native population, (b) have more

---

Administration does not immediately release these funds, they are eventually are rolled into the general funds of the federal government.

[41] Smith and Edmonston, *The New Americans*.

children, causing them to make greater use of public education, and (c) earn lower incomes, leading them to have lower tax payments and greater use of public assistance.

For the nation as a whole, the NRC estimated that in 1996 immigration imposed a short-run fiscal burden on the average U.S. native household of $200, or 0.2 percent of U.S. GDP.[42] In that year, the immigration surplus was about 0.1 percent of GDP.[43] A back of the envelope calculation then suggests that in the short run immigration in the mid-1990s reduced the annual income of U.S. residents by about 0.1 percent of GDP. Given the uncertainties involved in making this calculation, one should not put great stock in the fact that the resulting estimate is negative. The prediction error around the estimate, though unknown, is likely to be large, in which case the -0.1 percent estimate would be statistically indistinguishable from zero. Using this sort of analysis, we cannot say with much conviction whether the aggregate impact of immigration on the U.S. economy is positive or negative. What available evidence does suggest is that the total impact is small.

When considering reforms to U.S. immigration policy, it is not the total effect of immigration on the U.S. economy that matters but the impact of the immigrants who would be affected by the changes currently being considered in U.S. admission and enforcement policies. The immigrants that account for the negative fiscal impact of immigration in California and the United States as a whole are primarily individuals with low skill levels. This group includes legal immigrants (most of whom presumably entered the country on family-based immigration visas) and illegal immigrants. The Center for Immigration Studies (CIS), a think tank that advocates reducing immigration, has recently applied the NRC methodology to estimate the fiscal impact of illegal

---

[42] Going from a short-run to a long-run estimate of the fiscal cost of immigration can change the results. Immigrants are relatively young and far from their peak earning and taxpaying years. As immigrants age, their net fiscal contribution increases. Also, their children are likely to be more educated and to make greater tax contributions. The NRC estimates that the average immigrant admitted in 1990 would produce a net fiscal contribution of $80,000 over the next 300 years (in present discounted value terms), with the contribution depending on the individual's skill level. The long-run fiscal contribution is negative for low-skilled immigrants (less than a high school education) and positive for higher-skilled immigrants (more than a high school education). Going 300 years forward requires strong assumptions about the future economy. Even for the average immigrant, the annual net fiscal contribution is negative for the first twenty-five years after arriving in the United States. The long-run estimate assumes the federal government will ultimately raise taxes to bring the federal budget into balance. If this doesn't happen, the long-run fiscal contribution of the average immigrant would be negative. See Smith and Edmonston, *The New Americans*.
[43] Borjas, *Heaven's Door*.

immigration. The CIS finds that in 2002 illegal immigrants on net received $10 billion more in government benefits than they paid in taxes, a value equal to 0.1 percent of U.S. GDP in that year.[44] With unauthorized immigrants accounting for 5 percent of the U.S. labor force, U.S. residents would receive a surplus from illegal immigration of about 0.03 percent of GDP. Combining these two numbers, it appears that as of 2002 illegal immigration caused an annual income loss of 0.07 percent of U.S. GDP. Again, given the uncertainties surrounding this sort of calculation, one could not say with much confidence that this impact is statistically distinguishable from zero.

The net economic impact of immigration on the U.S. economy appears to be modest. Available evidence suggests that the immigration of high-skilled individuals has a small positive impact on the incomes of U.S. residents, while the arrival of low-skilled immigrants, either legal or illegal, has a small negative impact. Given that the estimates in question require strong assumptions and in the end are only a fraction of a percent of U.S. GDP, one cannot say that they differ significantly from zero. For the U.S. economy, immigration appears to be more or less a wash.

From an economic perspective, the question for policymakers then becomes whether the costs of halting illegal immigration would significantly outweigh the possible benefits. This paper has already discussed the benefits that come from having a flexible supply of low-skilled labor, which would be jeopardized by some of the reforms being considered. In addition, the enforcement costs of reducing the flow of illegal migrants are substantial and growing. President George W. Bush's budget proposal for 2008 calls for spending $13 billion to strengthen border security and immigration enforcement, including $1 billion to construct fences and undertake other security measures on the border with Mexico. Since 2001, Congress has increased funding for border security by 145 percent and immigration enforcement by 118 percent.[45]

For the sake of argument, take literally the estimate that illegal immigration was costing the economy the equivalent of 0.07 percent of GDP annually as of 2002. In that year, the Immigration and Naturalization Service spent $4.2 billion (or 0.04 percent of

---

[44] Camarota, *The High Cost of Cheap Labor*. The CIS estimates that in 2002 households headed by illegal immigrants paid taxes equal to $16 billion and imposed costs on the government equal to $26.3 billion. In that year, U.S. GDP was $10.47 trillion.

[45] See Office of Management and Budget, Department of Homeland Security, http://www.whitehouse.gov/omb/budget/fy2008/homeland.html.

GDP) on border and interior enforcement, including the detention and removal of illegal aliens, in a year in which half a million net new illegal immigrants entered the country.[46] The $13 billion in proposed border security spending for next year is already two-and-a-half times that figure at 0.10 percent of GDP. With the already huge increases in spending, the flow of illegal immigrants across the southern border (as measured by apprehensions) is estimated to have fallen by about 27 percent last year. How much money would be required to reduce illegal immigration to zero? Even far short of sealing the borders, the funds spent on extra enforcement would vastly exceed the income gained from eliminating the net fiscal transfer to households headed by illegal immigrants. One should keep in mind, however, that this cost-benefit calculation is based purely on the economic consequences of illegal immigration. There may be gains to increased border enforcement associated with enhanced national security that would justify the expense, but they are not economic gains.

While the aggregate impacts of both legal and illegal immigration are small, the intensity of the public debate about the economic impacts of immigration is not a reflection of its aggregate consequences. Business, which is the biggest winner from high levels of immigration, is the strongest defender of the status quo. Low-skilled workers and select high-skilled workers whose wages are depressed by immigration, at least in the short run, want to see tougher enforcement. Nationally, the less educated tend to be the most opposed to immigration, with their opposition being stronger in states with larger immigrant populations.[47]

Taxpayers in high-immigration states have also been vocal opponents of illegal immigration. States pay most of the costs of providing public services to immigrants, which include public education to immigrant children and Medicaid to poor immigrant households (whose U.S.-born children and naturalized members are eligible to receive such assistance).[48] The federal government, in contrast, appears to enjoy a net fiscal surplus from immigration.[49] Washington is responsible for many activities, including national defense and managing public lands, whose cost varies relatively little with the

---

[46] See the Budget of the United States Government at http://origin.www.gpoaccess.gov.
[47] Scheve and Slaughter, *Globalization and the Perceptions of American Workers.*
[48] Frank D. Bean and Gillian Stevens, *America's Newcomers and the Dynamics of Diversity* (New York: Russell Sage Foundation, 2005).
[49] Smith and Edmonston, *The New Americans.*

size of the population. Since immigrants (including many illegals) pay federal income and withholding taxes, the federal government enjoys an increase in revenue from immigration but does not incur much in the way of additional expenses, which are borne primarily at the state and local level. Part of the political opposition to immigration comes from the uneven burden sharing associated with labor inflows. Governors in high-immigration western states, regardless of their party affiliation, have been among the strongest critics of lax federal enforcement against illegal entry.

Results from public opinion surveys bear out this analysis. College graduates, while generally more supportive of immigration, are less supportive in states that have larger populations of low-skilled immigrants and more generous welfare policies, which in combination tend to produce larger tax burdens on high-income individuals.[50]

[50] Gordon H. Hanson, *Why Does Immigration Divide America? Public Finance and Political Opposition to Open Borders* (Washington, DC: Institute for International Economics, 2005); Gordon Hanson, Kenneth Scheve, and Matthew Slaughter, "Public Finance and Individual Preferences over Globalization Strategies," *Economics and Politics*, forthcoming.

REFORMING IMMIGRATION POLICY

The changes to U.S. immigration policy that Congress is contemplating are intended to slow illegal immigration, leaving legal permanent immigration and temporary immigration of high-skilled workers largely intact. If a bill can be passed, it will most likely tighten enforcement against illegal immigrants, expand the number of temporary work visas available to guest workers, and revise provisions for illegal immigrants to obtain legal status. How would such a policy reform alter immigration's impact on the U.S. economy?

One issue on which most members of Congress agree is that border and interior enforcement should be expanded. At current enforcement levels, as many as 400,000 new illegal immigrants are probably still entering the country on net each year, and halting that flow will require a further increase in the already substantial resources devoted to the task.

The expenditures on border enforcement (more than 0.1 percent of GDP) are already greater than the fiscal benefits of reducing illegal immigration (less than 0.1 percent of GDP). This is not to say border and interior enforcement should be ignored. Existing legislative proposals also contain provisions to redirect funds toward expanding the electronic verification of employee eligibility and reassigning border patrol personnel to locations where their presence may be a greater deterrent to illegal entry. These or other reallocations of existing spending may be effective in reducing illegal immigration. Currently, U.S. employers, by virtue of asking workers for identification at the time of their hiring, can plausibly deny having knowingly hired illegal immigrants. A system of electronic verification would potentially eliminate plausible deniability, placing a greater burden on employers to screen out workers who are unauthorized for employment. But by any measure, halting illegal immigration is likely to be a net drain on the U.S. economy.

President Bush and some members of Congress also advocate expanding the number of temporary work visas available to low-skilled immigrants to absorb illegal immigrants already in the country reduce the incentives for future illegal migration.

Among the measures currently under consideration, the maximum contemplated increase in temporary work visas is around 320,000 per year. With the combined number of H-2A (manual agricultural laborers) and H-2B (manual nonagricultural) visas currently at 66,000 per year, this would mean expanding the number of low-skilled guest workers in the United States by up to five times.

The proposed change in the number of guest workers may seem like a large increase. However, one must keep in mind that guest workers are by definition temporary. Expanding the annual number of visas by 260,000 or so does not mean that 260,000 new permanent workers enter the economy each year. Under a guest worker program, most or all of the guest workers admitted in one year would have to return to their home countries sometime in the future. Suppose, for instance, each guest worker were given a one-year visa, which could be renewed up to two times (such that the maximum length of stay for a temporary worker would be three years). Even if all guest workers elected to renew their visas for the maximum period allowable, which appears unlikely given experience with the H-1 program, the long-run increase in the stock of foreign workers in the U.S. economy would be only 780,000 individuals, roughly equal to the number of net new illegal immigrants that enter the United States every two years.[51] The apparent massive increase in the guest worker program Congress is envisioning would only absorb a few years' worth of current inflows of illegal immigrants. Absent substantial increases in enforcement, it is difficult to believe that a guest worker program on this scale would do much to dent the long-run demand for illegal labor.

Beyond the magnitude of labor inflows, it is crucial to recognize that one attractive feature of unauthorized workers for U.S. employers is their flexibility. Illegal immigrants fill jobs for which the supply of U.S. native workers is in decline, appear in larger numbers when the U.S. economy is booming (and Mexico's is not), and move between employers and regions of the country according to changes in the demand for labor. Depending on how temporary work visas are awarded and defined, new legal guest workers may have none of these qualities. Under the current H-2 visa program U.S. employers must apply for guest workers well in advance of when they would like them to

---

[51] Lowell, "H-1B Temporary Workers."

arrive, establish that no U.S. workers are available to fill the designated jobs, and demonstrate that they are paying prevailing wages. Once in the country, guest workers are tied to the employers who have sponsored them, leaving them unable to take advantage of new opportunities that may arise. The advance planning, occupational limitations, and bureaucratic hurdles involved in hiring guest workers reduce their value to the U.S. economy relative to comparably skilled unauthorized workers.

If immigration reform has the effect of replacing flexible and mobile illegal workers with inflexible and immobile guest workers, it would be likely to diminish the immigration surplus that foreign labor generates for the U.S. economy. Existing employment practices support this reasoning. Low-skilled temporary immigrants on H-2 visas have been in strongest demand by the tourist industry, in which business knows its bookings in advance and is able to plan for how many workers will be needed. In contrast, workers with H-2 visas have been in much less demand in volatile industries such as construction.

To succeed, a temporary immigration program would have to allow for flexibility and speed in hiring. Existing hiring of illegal immigrants much more closely resembles practices in the rapidly expanding U.S. temporary employment industry than it does employment of H-2 visa holders. Temporary employment agencies match a large stock of workers to an ever change pool of employers. Given the difficulties that the Department of Homeland Security has had in tracking legal immigrants in the country, there would be obvious complications in implementing a program that allowed temporary immigrant workers to be matched to multiple employers in succession. However, without such a dynamic matching process, a temporary immigration program could not effectively respond to the rapid pace of change in U.S. labor market conditions, which would limit the interest of U.S. employers in utilizing the system. Few existing legislative proposals offer specifics for how new temporary immigration programs would be implemented. Crucial to any program's success would be incorporating features that encourage the active participation of U.S. employers.[52]

---

[52] Another concern is that if temporary legal immigrants were allowed to bring their families with them, the new immigrants may choose to remain in the country after their visas expire, regardless of their legal status. See Martin, "U.S. Employment-Based Admissions." A new temporary legal immigration program could mirror the effects of the Hart-Cellar Act, which redefined U.S. admission policies in the 1960s to make

The most divisive issue surrounding immigration reform is whether to offer illegal immigrants an opportunity to legalize their status. One view is that there is no other means, save politically unacceptable mass deportations, to reduce the number of illegal aliens in the country. Another view is that legalizing unauthorized entrants rewards individuals who have broken the law and creates an incentive for continued illegal immigration in the future. Opponents to legalization cite the surge in illegal immigration after the IRCA amnesty in the late 1980s as evidence that granting legal status to illegal aliens does not solve the problem.

The illegal immigrant population—currently at about 12 million individuals—has reached a level at which any attempt to diminish its size would require prolonged effort. Ignoring the humanitarian and practical difficulties involved in encouraging illegal immigrants to leave the country, what would be the economic impact? Sending all illegal immigrants home would reduce the U.S. labor force by 5 percent and the low-skilled U.S. labor force (workers with less than a high school education) by 10 percent or more. In 2005, illegal immigrants accounted for 24 percent of workers employed in farming, 17 percent in cleaning, 14 percent in construction, and 12 percent in food preparation.[53] Losing this labor would likely increase prices for many types of non-traded goods and services, increase wages for low-skilled resident labor, decrease incomes of employers that hire these workers, and increase the incomes of taxpayers that pay for the public services these individuals use. The net impact of these changes would be small, although in some regions and industries the dislocation caused by the labor outflow would be considerable.

If, instead, illegal immigrants were allowed to remain in the country and obtain legal residence visas, the economic impact would depend on the rights granted to these individuals. In the short run, the economic impact of legalization would likely be minimal. Illegal immigrants are already allowed to send their children to public schools and to receive emergency medical care. The U.S.-born children of illegal immigrants are eligible to receive Medicaid, school lunches, and other forms of public assistance directed toward children. Even as legal residents, existing illegal immigrants would be ineligible

---

family reunification the primary motivation for entry and which has served as a vehicle for substantial inflows of new immigrants.

[53] Passel, "Estimates of the Size and Characteristics of the Undocumented Population."

to receive much in the way of public assistance until they became U.S. citizens, a process that would take at least five years after receipt of a green card. Under some proposals, the path to citizenship for illegal immigrants would take ten years or more, implying that the full fiscal consequences of legalization would not be felt for at least a decade. For the immigrants themselves, research on the IRCA amnesty suggests legalization would lead to higher wages and more opportunity for occupational advancement. Sherrie A. Kossoudji and Deborah A. Cobb-Clark compare wages for illegal immigrants before and after they obtained green cards under IRCA.[54] Between 1989 and 1992, average hourly earnings for newly legalized immigrant men rose by 6 percent relative to earnings for other Latino men (controlling for the observable characteristics of these workers). Based on further analysis, Kossoudji and Cobb-Clark suggest the wage penalty from illegality is due to unauthorized workers being unable to move between occupations.

There are no easy answers to U.S. immigration problems. Any substantial reform to existing policy would invite intense opposition from some quarter. While economic analysis may not identify the ideal reform package that would both improve national welfare and garner majority political support, it does help identify paths that would be likely to make the country worse off. Among the policy changes that would be likely to lower the incomes of U.S. residents are a large increase in spending on border or interior enforcement or the conversion of illegal workers to legal guest workers who cannot be hired quickly or move easily between jobs. Interestingly, the near-term economic consequences of legalization, the most bitterly contested aspect of policy reform, appear to be limited. The fiscal consequences of providing illegal immigrants with a path to citizenship would not be felt for over a decade and could be controlled by defining the types of government benefits to which legalized immigrants are eligible.

---

[54] Sherrie A. Kossoudji and Deborah A. Cobb-Clark, "Coming out of the Shadows: Learning about Legal Status and Wages from the Legalized Population," *Journal of Labor Economics*, Vol. 20, No. 3 (July 2002), pp. 598–628.

FINAL CONSIDERATIONS

The contentiousness surrounding immigration deters many politicians from tackling the issue. While specific groups of workers, employers, and taxpayers may have much to gain or lose if policies governing illegal immigration are changed, the aggregate economic effects of policy reform do not appear to be large. In revising admission and entry restrictions, members of Congress face the unenviable choice of dramatically altering the welfare of a few voters while having a nearly imperceptible effect on aggregate welfare. This dilemma may explain why it has taken policymakers so long to get around to addressing illegal immigration. For over a decade, the net inflow of unauthorized entrants has been close to 500,000 individuals a year. Yet, it is only in the last year or two that Congress has felt compelled to reexamine the issue.

In weighing the various proposals under discussion, policymakers would do well to separate the distributional impacts of immigration from its aggregate effects. No initiative under consideration has the potential to substantially increase the overall income of U.S. residents. Because the aggregate gains or losses are small, any new policy that requires a major outlay of funds would be likely to lower U.S. economic well-being. In a rush to secure U.S. borders, some policymakers insist that major efforts are needed to prevent continued illegal inflows from abroad. While the goals of reducing illegality and establishing greater border control are laudable, it would be difficult to justify massive new spending in terms of its economic return.

Illegal immigration is a persistent phenomenon in part because it has a strong economic rationale. Low-skilled workers are increasingly scarce in the United States, while still abundant in Mexico, Central America, and elsewhere. Impeding illegal immigration, without creating other avenues for legal entry, would conflict with market forces that push for moving labor from low-productivity, low-wage countries to the high-productivity, high-wage U.S. labor market. The acceptance of these market pressures is behind proposals for a large-scale expansion of temporary legal immigration. For many elected officials, temporary legal immigration is still immigration, so they have sought to regulate guest workers in a manner that insulates U.S. labor markets from economic repercussions. But highly regulated inflows of temporary low-skilled foreign labor would be unlikely to attract much interest from U.S. employers. If foreign labor wants to come to the United States and U.S. business wants to hire these workers, then creating cumbersome legal channels through which labor could flow would give employers an incentive to eschew the new guest workers and continue to hire unauthorized workers instead. Were new legislation to combine stronger border and interior enforcement with an unattractive guest worker program, it would be pitting policy reform against itself, with only one of these components likely to survive in the long run.

What provisions might a successful guest worker program entail? To reduce demand for illegal-immigrant labor, a new visa program would have to mimic current beneficial aspects of illegal immigration. Employers would have to be able to hire the types of workers they desire. One way to achieve this would be for the Department of Homeland Security to sanction the creation of global temp agencies, in which U.S. employers posted advertisements for jobs and foreign workers applied to fill these jobs. As with the legal temporary labor market in the United States, intermediaries would likely arise to provide the services of screening workers and evaluating their applications. With illegal labor, screening happens informally. Illegal immigrants from Mexico help friends or relatives get jobs in the United States by vouching for their qualifications. Informal job networks help integrate the U.S. and Mexican labor markets. Formalizing these networks by allowing employers and employees in the two countries to match legally would deepen U.S.-Mexico integration.

Matching foreign workers to U.S. employers efficiently would require flexibility in the number of guest workers admitted. During U.S. economic expansions, there would be more employers searching for foreign workers. Similarly, during economic contractions in Mexico and elsewhere, there would be more foreign workers advertising their availability to take jobs abroad. Keeping the number of visas fixed over time, as is the case now, means that during boom times U.S. employers have a stronger incentive to seek out illegal labor. One way to make the number of visas granted sensitive to market signals would be to auction the right to hire a guest worker to U.S. employers. Congress would determine the appropriate number of visas to issue under normal macroeconomic conditions. The auction price that clears the market would reflect the supply of and demand for foreign guest workers. Increases in the auction price would signal the need to expand the number of visas available; decreases in the price would indicate that the number of visas could be reduced. By setting a range in which the auction price for a visa right would fluctuate, Congress could ensure that flows of guest workers into the U.S. economy would help stave off demand for unauthorized labor.

Perhaps the most important provision of any new visa program would be to allow guest workers to move between jobs in the United States. Currently, H-1 and H-2 visa holders are tied to the employer that sponsors them. Without mobility between employers, guest workers would lack the attractiveness of illegal laborers. They would also be exposed to abuse by unscrupulous bosses. One way to facilitate mobility for guest workers would be to allow existing visa holders to apply for new job postings, along with prospective guest workers abroad.[55] U.S. employers could then hire either existing guest workers or new guest workers, depending on who best matched their needs. In this way, guest workers could move between industries and regions of the country in response to changes in economic conditions, much as illegal laborers do now. What would differ between illegal and temporary legal employment is that the latter would enjoy the protection of U.S. labor laws and regulations.

None of the provisions discussed would be easy to implement, either administratively or politically. However, absent a bold redesign of U.S. guest worker programs, temporary legal immigrants would be unlikely to displace illegal labor.

In the Immigration Reform and Control Act of 1986, Congress voted to increase enforcement without creating a mechanism for the continued legal inflow of low-skilled labor. Under steady pressure from business, immigration authorities ultimately gutted or redirected IRCA's major enforcement provisions. The end result was that illegal labor has continued to find a way into the country. As Congress again wrestles with immigration reform, one would hope that it will pay heed to the failures of IRCA by designing a framework that allows for the dynamic participation of legal immigrant workers in the U.S. economy. Otherwise, the United States is likely to find itself with even larger illegal populations in the very near future.

---

[55] Hiring an existing guest worker would require the new employer to compensate the worker's existing employer by paying the amortized price of the visa right purchased when the worker was originally hired.

REFERENCES

Auerbach, Alan J. and Philip Oreopoulos. "Analyzing the Fiscal Impact of U.S. Immigration." *American Economic Review*, Vol. 89, No. 2 (May 1999), pp. 176–80.

Bean, Frank D. and Gillian Stevens. *America's Newcomers and the Dynamics of Diversity.* New York: Russell Sage Foundation, 2005.

Borjas, George J. *Heaven's Door: Immigration Policy and the American Economy.* Princeton, NJ: Princeton University Press, 1999.

Borjas, George J. "The Labor Demand Curve is Downward Sloping: Reexamining the Impact of Immigration on the Labor Market." *Quarterly Journal of Economics*, Vol. 118, No. 4 (June 2003), pp. 1335–74.

Buchanan, Patrick J. *State of Emergency: The Third World Invasion and Conquest of America.* New York: Thomas Dunne, 2006.

Buchanan, Patrick J. "U.S. Pays the High Price of Empire." *Los Angeles Times*, September 18, 2001.

Bureau of International Labor Affairs. *Effects of the Immigration Reform and Control Act: Characteristics and Labor Market Behavior of the Legalized Population Five Years Following Legalization.* Washington, DC: U.S. Department of Labor, 1996.

Calavita, Kitty. *Inside the State: The Bracero Program, Immigration and the I.N.S.* New York: Routledge, Chapman and Hall, 1992.

Camarota, Steven A. *The Open Door: How Militant Islamic Terrorists Entered and Remained in the United States.* Center for Immigration Studies Paper No. 21 (2002).

Camarota, Steven A. *The High Cost of Cheap Labor: Illegal Immigration and the Federal Budget.* Center for Immigration Studies, 2004.

Card, David. "Is the New Immigration Really so Bad?" NBER Working Paper No. 11547 (August 2005).

Card, David and Ethan G. Lewis. "The Diffusion of Mexican Immigrants During the 1990s: Explanations and Impacts." In George J. Borjas, ed., *Mexican Immigration to the United States.* Chicago: University of Chicago and National Bureau of Economic Research, forthcoming.

Cornelius, Wayne A. "Death at the Border: Efficacy and Unintended Consequences of U.S. Immigration Control Policy." *Population and Development Review*, Vol. 27, No. 4 (December 2001), pp. 661–85.

Cortes, Patricia. "The Effect of Low-Skilled Immigration on U.S. Prices: Evidence from CPI Data." Mimeo, MIT, November 2005.

Hanson, Gordon H. *Why Does Immigration Divide America? Public Finance and Political Opposition to Open Borders*. Washington, DC: Institute for International Economics, 2005.

Hanson, Gordon H. "Illegal Migration from Mexico to the United States." *Journal of Economic Literature*, Vol. 44, No. 4 (December 2006), pp. 869–924.

Hanson, Gordon H. and Antonio Spilimbergo. "Illegal Immigration, Border Enforcement, and Relative Wages: Evidence from Apprehensions at the U.S.-Mexico Border." *American Economic Review*, Vol. 89, No. 5 (December 1999), pp. 1337–57.

Hanson, Gordon H., Kenneth F. Scheve, and Matthew J. Slaughter. "Public Finance and Individual Preferences over Globalization Strategies." *Economics and Politics*, forthcoming.

Hollifield, James F. and Valerie F. Hunt. "Immigrants, Markets, and Rights: The US as an Emerging Migration State." Paper prepared for presentation at the Migration Ethnicity Meeting (MEM) at IZA in Bonn, Germany, May 13–16, 2006.

Huntington, Samuel P. *Who Are We? The Challenges to America's National Identity*. New York: Simon and Schuster, 2004.

Jasso, Guillermina and Mark R. Rosenzweig. "Selection Criteria and the Skill Composition of Immigrants: A Comparative Analysis of Australian and US Employment Immigration." Mimeo, New York University and Yale University, 2005.

Katz, Lawrence F. and David H. Autor, "Changes in the Wage Structure and Earnings Inequality." In Orley Ashenfelter and David Card, eds., *Handbook of Labor Economics, Vol. 3A*, Amsterdam: Elsevier Science, 1999, pp. 1463–1555.

Kossoudji, Sherrie A. and Deborah A. Cobb-Clark. "Coming out of the Shadows: Learning about Legal Status and Wages from the Legalized Population." *Journal of Labor Economics*, Vol. 20, No. 3 (July 2002), pp. 598–628.

Lowell, B. Lindsay. "H-1B Temporary Workers: Estimating the Population." Mimeo, Institute for the Study of International Migration, Georgetown University, 2000.

Martin, David A. "Twilight Statuses: A Closer Examination of the Unauthorized Population." Migration Policy Institute Policy Brief No. 2 (June 2005).

Martin, Susan. "U.S. Employment-Based Admissions: Permanent and Temporary." Migration Policy Institute Policy Brief No. 15 (January 2006).

Passel, Jeffrey S. "Estimates of the Size and Characteristics of the Undocumented Population." Pew Hispanic Center, 2006.

Scheve, Kenneth F. and Matthew J. Slaughter. *Globalization and the Perceptions of American Workers.* Washington, DC: Institute for International Economics, 2001.

Smith, James P. and Barry Edmonston, eds. *The New Americans: Economic, Demographic, and Fiscal Effects of Immigration.* Washington, DC: National Academy Press, 1997.

U.S. Department of Homeland Security. "2005 Yearbook of Immigration Statistics." Office of Immigration Statistics, 2006.

U.S. Government Accountability Office. "Immigration Enforcement: Preliminary Observations on Employment Verification and Worksite Enforcement." GAO-05-822T (June 21, 2005).

Van Hook, Jennifer, Weiwei Zhang, Frank D. Bean, and Jeffrey S. Passel. "Foreign-Born Emigration: A New Approach and Estimates Based on Matched CPS Files." *Demography*, Vol. 43, No. 2 (May 2006), pp. 361–82.

Zimmerman, Wendy and Karen C. Tumlin. "Patchwork Policies: State Assistance for Immigrants under Welfare Reform." Urban Institute Paper No. 21 (April 1999).

ABOUT THE AUTHOR

Gordon H. Hanson is the director of the Center on Pacific Economies and professor of economics at University of California, San Diego, where he holds faculty positions in the Graduate School of International Relations and Pacific Studies and the department of economics. Professor Hanson is also a research associate at the National Bureau of Economic Research and coeditor of the *Journal of Development Economics*. He obtained his BA in economics from Occidental College in 1986 and his PhD in economics from MIT in 1992. Prior to joining UCSD in 2001, he was on the economics faculty at the University of Michigan (1998–2001) and at the University of Texas (1992–1998). Professor Hanson has published extensively in the top academic venues of the economics discipline. His current research examines the international migration of high-skilled labor, the causes of Mexican migration to the United States, the consequences of immigration on labor-market outcomes for African-Americans, the relationship between business cycles and foreign outsourcing, and international trade in motion pictures. In recent work, he has studied the impact of globalization on wages, the origins of political opposition to immigration, and the implications of China's growth for the export performance of Mexico and other developing countries. His most recent book is *Why Does Immigration Divide America? Public Finance and Political Opposition to Open Borders* (Institute for International Economics, 2005).

ADVISORY COMMITTEE FOR

THE ECONOMIC LOGIC OF ILLEGAL IMMIGRATION

Mark A. Anderson
THE WESSEL GROUP, INC.

Frank D. Bean
UNIVERSITY OF CALIFORNIA, IRVINE

Michael J. Christenson
CA, INC.

Jose W. Fernandez
LATHAM & WATKINS LLP

James F. Hollifield
SOUTHERN METHODIST UNIVERSITY

Stephen L. Kass
CARTER, LEDYARD & MILBURN LLP

Moushumi M. Khan
LAW OFFICES OF MOUSHUMI M.
KHAN

F. Ray Marshall
UNIVERSITY OF TEXAS AT AUSTIN

Susan F. Martin
GEORGETOWN UNIVERSITY

Prachi Mishra
INTERNATIONAL MONETARY FUND

Robert J. Murray
THE CNA CORPORATION

David Perez
PALLADIUM EQUITY PARTNERS

Michael Piore
MASSACHUSETTS INSTITUTE OF
TECHNOLOGY

Mark R. Rosenzweig
YALE UNIVERSITY

Gerald L. Warren
SAN DIEGO UNION-TRIBUNE

Note: Council Special Reports reflect the judgments and recommendations of the author(s). They do not necessarily represent the views of members of the advisory committee, whose involvement in no way should be interpreted as an endorsement of the report by either themselves or the organizations with which they are affiliated.

RECENT COUNCIL SPECIAL REPORTS
SPONSORED BY THE COUNCIL ON FOREIGN RELATIONS

The United States and the WTO Dispute Settlement System
Robert Z. Lawrence; CSR No. 25, March 2007
A Maurice R. Greenberg Center for Geoeconomic Studies Report

Bolivia on the Brink
Eduardo A. Gamarra; CSR No. 24, February 2007
A Center for Preventive Action Report

After the Surge: The Case for U.S. Military Disengagement from Iraq
Steven N. Simon; CSR No. 23, February 2007

Darfur and Beyond: What Is Needed to Prevent Mass Atrocities
Lee Feinstein; CSR No. 22, January 2007

Avoiding Conflict in the Horn of Africa: U.S. Policy Toward Ethiopia and Eritrea
Terrence Lyons; CSR No. 21, December 2006
A Center for Preventive Action Report

Living with Hugo: U.S. Policy Toward Hugo Chávez's Venezuela
Richard Lapper; CSR No. 20, November 2006
A Center for Preventive Action Report

Reforming U.S. Patent Policy: Getting the Incentives Right
Keith E. Maskus; CSR No. 19, November 2006
A Maurice R. Greenberg Center for Geoeconomic Studies Report

Foreign Investment and National Security: Getting the Balance Right
Alan P. Larson, David M. Marchick; CSR No. 18, July 2006
A Maurice R. Greenberg Center for Geoeconomic Studies Report

Challenges for a Postelection Mexico: Issues for U.S. Policy
Pamela K. Starr; CSR No. 17, June 2006 (web-only release) and November 2006

U.S.-India Nuclear Cooperation: A Strategy for Moving Forward
Michael A. Levi and Charles D. Ferguson; CSR No. 16, June 2006

Generating Momentum for a New Era in U.S.-Turkey Relations
Steven A. Cook and Elizabeth Sherwood-Randall; CSR No. 15, June 2006

Peace in Papua: Widening a Window of Opportunity
Blair A. King; CSR No. 14, March 2006
A Center for Preventive Action Report

Neglected Defense: Mobilizing the Private Sector to Support Homeland Security
Stephen E. Flynn and Daniel B. Prieto; CSR No. 13, March 2006

To purchase a printed copy, call the Brookings Institution Press: 800-537-5487.
Note: Council Special Reports are available to download from the Council's website, CFR.org.
For more information, contact publications@cfr.org.